Contemporary

SOCCER

Klaus Ruege

Contemporary Books, Inc.
Chicago

Library of Congress Cataloging in Publication Data

Ruege, Klaus.
   Contemporary soccer.

   Includes index.
   1. Soccer.   I. Title.
GV943.R73   1978   796.33'42   77-91172
ISBN 0-8092-7556-2
ISBN 0-8092-7656-9 pbk.

Published by Contemporary Books, Inc.
180 North Michigan Avenue, Chicago, Illinois 60601
Manufactured in the United States of America
Library of Congress Catalog Card Number: 77-91172
International Standard Book Number: 0-8092-7556-2 (cloth)
                                              0-8092-7656-9 (paper)

Published simultaneously in Canada by
Beaverbooks
150 Lesmill Road
Don Mills, Ontario M3B 2T5
Canada

Contents

Acknowledgments

The author would like to thank the many kind friends and associates who helped to put this book together. Special thanks go to Gigi Izquierdo and the staff of Izquierdo Studios for the diagrams that illustrate the book; Wayne Pirmann, Michigan Soccer School Director, for his helpful comments; David Burns of the Burns Sports Celebrity Service, Inc., for his encouragement and wise counsel; and to the various North American Soccer League executives for their helpful assistance—including John Chaffetz of the Los Angeles Aztecs, Tom Mertens of the San Jose Earthquakes, Jim Trecker of the Cosmos, and Jim Walker of the Chicago Sting.

In addition, the author wishes to express his appreciation to the following NASL clubs for providing photographs: the Los Angeles Aztecs (Photos 1 and 5), the Cosmos (Photo 7), and the San Jose Earthquakes (Photos 3 and 4).

Photo 1:   George Best of Los Angeles dribbles past Pele.

Introduction

Nothing quite like it has been seen before in American sports—a relatively unknown pastime has mushroomed in less than ten years into a nationwide sport. Thousands of men and women have been caught up in the fervent pursuit of a round ball. Soccer has arrived, and all over the United States new leagues are sprouting up as the sport takes a firm grip on the Saturday and Sunday afternoon sporting scene.

Soccer's most phenomenal growth has been among the youth of America, particularly in the 8-to-14 age bracket. The latest estimate shows nearly 2 million youngsters playing in organized leagues as compared to fewer than 200,000 in 1968.

Professional soccer has also surged ahead since the late sixties with a steady rise in playing standards and attendance. Crowds of 30,000 and 40,000 are not uncommon sights in such cities as Dallas, Minneapolis, New York, Portland, St. Louis, Seattle, and Tampa. In 1977 pro soccer proved beyond all doubt it had come of age when 77,691 fans were attracted to the Giants Stadium to see the Cosmos play the Fort Lauderdale Strikers.

What all these Americans have discovered (approximately 50 years later than the rest of the world) is that soccer has something to entice everyone: for the spectator it has rules that are easily understood and fast-paced action that is a pleasure to view; and for the player it demands only inexpensive equipment, sets no height or weight requirements, and best of all is undoubtedly the finest team sport for keeping one's body in tip-top shape. When one considers that the average-size soccer field is 110 by 75 yards and that the game is 90 minutes in duration, divided into two 45-minute halves, one can well understand why soccer players are considered the fittest athletes in the world.

Although Chapter 5 deals with the 17 rules (or laws of the game, to give them their official title) it would be helpful for the beginner to read a brief discussion here of some of the more important features of the game.

First of all, soccer is different from any other sport in that one player, the goalkeeper, has a set of rules different from that of his or her teammates. Whereas all other players commit an infringement (or foul) whenever they touch the ball with their hands or arms, the goalkeeper is able to play the ball with any part of the body. So, out of 11 players on the team, 10 of them may, at one time or another, kick, head (use the head to propel the ball), or trap the ball (stop or cushion it with either the feet, thighs, waist, chest, or head), while the goalkeeper may, in addition, catch, punch, or carry the ball with his hands.

Another peculiarity of soccer is the lack of time-outs. The only time the game is stopped is when an injury occurs. The referee is the sole arbiter in deciding whether the injury is serious enough to warrant stopping the flow of the game.

It is the referee who also must distinguish between two types of infringements, nine of which are considered more serious and result in direct free kicks against the offending team, and six less serious, with indirect free kicks resulting. If a direct free kick is awarded to the offensive team in its opponent's penalty area it becomes a penalty kick and is taken from the penalty spot with only the kicker and the goalkeeper permitted in the penalty area at the time of the kick. (For a diagram of a soccer field, see Figure 5.2.)

The referee leaves it to his two linesmen to indicate when the ball has gone out of play. When it goes over one of the two touchlines (sidelines), play is restarted by means of a throw-in. When the ball goes over one of the two goal lines, either the offensive team gets a corner kick (if the ball was last touched by a defending player) or the defensive team is awarded a goal kick (if the ball was last touched by an offensive player).

The object of the game of soccer, of course, is to score more goals than one's opponents. Teams try to achieve this object in a variety of ways. Some will employ their ten outfield players in a 4-2-4 formation (four defenders, two midfielders, and four forwards. Others, more defensive-minded, will pack their backline with five defenders helped by three midfielders, thus leaving only two forwards to attempt breakaways. Then there are those who begin the game with four forwards but pull nearly everyone back into a defensive shell once they have scored a goal. Soccer has always been an explosive, all-action game but modern soccer has added tactical and countertactical devices that force the players to utilize not only their skills and techniques but also their brains.

For the spectators, soccer, particularly professional soccer, offers an abundance of drama, thrills, individual artistry, and sophisticated teamwork. In the professional North American Soccer League one can see some of the world's best players. Stars of the caliber of George Best of the Los Angeles Aztecs, Franz Beckenbauer and Giorgio

Chinaglia of the Cosmos, Rodney Marsh of the Tampa Bay Rowdies, and Willie Morgan of the Chicago Sting can make viewing almost as interesting as playing.

But playing the game is really what any sport is all about, and soccer is no exception. The view from the bleachers may well be exhilarating but it pales when compared to active participation on the field. Whatever their contribution—be it scoring the winning goal or committing a serious blunder—the millions of players throughout the world still are happiest being a part of a game of soccer.

But for all of you who are just beginning to learn about the universal game, budding star and spectator alike, I hope this book acts as a spur to prompt you to take an active part in the fascinating world of soccer. I feel confident that, once you get the soccer bug, you will never get it out of your system.

Photo 2: Young Americans enjoy the action of soccer.

1

Learning the skills of ball control

To really enjoy playing soccer all beginners must learn to control the ball not only with the feet but also with the thighs, the chest, the head, and at times with just about every part of the body. Only the hands and arms are not brought directly into play as the beginner attempts complete mastery of the ball. Although some players seem to have a natural talent for remarkable ball control, most of the skills involved are perfected by only one thing: practice. George Best, Rodney Marsh, Franz Beckenbauer, and other top stars of the NASL all had to work hard when they were young to develop their ball-juggling skills. Even today they practice regularly.

Soccer being essentially a kicking game, it is vitally important that each player purchase a pair of shoes that fits comfortably. There is a wide selection on today's growing soccer market; manufacturers of name brands like Adidas, Gola, Puma, and others offer soccer shoes costing as high as $35 and as low as $8. Whatever price you decide to pay, make certain the shoes fit snugly.

1

If you buy low-cost shoes, try to get those that have the all-weather molded rubber cleats. With the more expensive shoes you will get interchangeable cleats. The advantage in having interchangeable cleats is that not only can they be changed to suit the weather conditions but they can also be unscrewed and replaced when worn out. If you select the interchangeable type, use rubber cleats for hard ground and either leather or plastic for wet and muddy fields. In addition, remember to use longer cleats for the muddy field and shorter ones when the field is dry.

When you're wearing a comfortable pair of shoes and perhaps a pair of shin pads underneath your socks, you're ready to go onto the field and practice the skills.

Kicking

Unlike American football, kicking in soccer seldom involves the toes. For over 100 years players have understood that the toe kick, which employs the small pointed part of the shoe, is far too inaccurate and uncontrollable. Three other types of kicks are used instead: the instep kick, which employs the large area from the top of the ankle down to the top of the toes; the inside-of-the-foot kick, which brings into play the long stretch of foot from the heel to the side of the big toe; and the outside-of-the-foot kick, which uses most of the outside of the foot.

Common to all types of kicks are the following basic principles:

1. Keep your eyes on the ball
2. Position the nonkicking foot in the correct spot alongside the ball
3. Balance your body on the nonkicking foot
4. Strike the ball with the correct part of the foot
5. Follow through with the kicking leg after striking the ball

The instep kick

The most common of all kicks, the instep kick can be used for both passing and shooting. The toes are pointed down so that the top part of the foot strikes the ball. The foot is also turned outward to enable the kicker to use the inside part of the instep as well.

THE LOW INSTEP KICK. When one wishes to pass a ball along the ground or to try a low shot at goal another type of instep kick is used than when one is attempting a lofted pass or a shot over the goalkeeper's head. In order to keep the ball low the player must keep the nonkicking foot alongside the ball. The knee of the kicking leg must be over the ball, and the instep must make contact with the center of the ball.

As in all instep kicks the approach to the ball is made from a slight angle so that all of the instep meets the ball. The kicking leg swings back and into the ball for added power and straightens out during the follow-through.

THE LOFTED INSTEP KICK. To send the ball up into the air the nonkicking foot is placed a few inches behind the ball. The kicking foot hits the lower part of the ball with part of the instep getting underneath the ball. In addition, the follow-through of the kicking leg is longer and higher than in the low instep kick.

The volley

The instep is also used for the high or low volley, half volley, and overhead volley kicks. Which of the kicks is executed depends on the height of the ball above the ground when it arrives. Although the action to be taken is similar to the basic instep kick, allowance must be made for the difference in height when contact is made.

Figure 1.1: Low instep kick

4

Figure 1.2: Lofted instep kick

THE LOW VOLLEY.   As Figure 1.3 shows, to keep the ball low the toes are pointed down and the knee is over the ball at time of contact. The follow-through is limited.

THE HIGH VOLLEY.   This kick, on the other hand, has a long follow-through and contact is made with the foot swinging up into the ball. Note also in Figure 1.4 how the body is learning backward and how the knee is positioned in contrast to the low volley.

THE HALF VOLLEY.   One of the most difficult kicks for beginners to master, the half volley is used for balls that are beginning to rise from a bounce, preferably no more than a few inches. The toe again is pointed down with the knee and the body leaning over the ball.

THE OVERHEAD VOLLEY (OR SCISSORS KICK).   Kicking an overhead volley is another elusive skill for many beginners since it entails not only kicking the ball in midair but also falling backward at the same time. The instep makes contact with

Figure 1.3: Low volley   **Figure 1.4:** High volley

Figure 1.5: Overhead volley

the ball and the body drops to the ground, with the hands, arms, and shoulders breaking the fall. The secret of the successful overhead volley is in the strong liftoff of the kicking foot so that the nonkicking foot goes up into the air first, followed then by the kicking foot in a scissors-like' action.

Using the inside of the foot

THE KICK. As the name implies, the inside-of-the-foot kick involves all the area between the big toe and the ankle. With such a large part of the foot coming into contact with the ball it is not surprising that this is the most accurate of all kicks. The one drawback to the inside-of-the-foot kick is

7

that it lacks the power of the instep kick and is therefore not used for long passes or long shots.

Unlike the instep kick, this kick involves little back-swing as the foot approaches the ball. The toes are not pointed down, and there is a limited follow-through of approximately 10 to 12 inches. To execute a correct inside-of-the-foot kick the player should raise his kicking foot two or three inches off the ground so that it will strike the ball in its center. If you wish to kick the ball low you will have to keep your body over the ball. For a lofted kick, lean backward.

THE VOLLEY. Another kick that the beginner should learn is the inside-of-the-foot volley. Perfect for handling balls that come at you below the knee, this kick is used for accurate passing or shooting when you would rather not attempt the

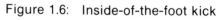

Figure 1.6: Inside-of-the-foot kick   Figure 1.7: Inside-of-the-foot vol-
ley

more powerful volley kick. As Figure 1.7 suggests, there is a short backswing and little follow-through when the leg is correctly positioned.

Other kicks

THE OUTSIDE-OF-THE-FOOT KICK. This kick used to be restricted to short passes but in recent years coaches and players alike have come to recognize how valuable it can be for quick shots at goal. The lack of a backswing makes it a perfect weapon near the goalmouth (the area immediately in

Figure 1.8: Outside-of-the-foot kick

front of the goal). To execute this kick the foot is turned inward, enabling the player to make contact with the ball with the outside of the foot as in Figure 1.8.

THE CHIP KICK. Whenever you wish to make a ball rise sharply off the ground, use the chip kick (or chip). Similar to a chip shot in golf, the chip kick is sharp and quick, with a short backswing and very little follow-through. It is easier to perform when the ball is coming toward you, but with practice even a beginner can learn quickly how to chip a stationary ball. Two important points to keep in mind with the chip are that the kicking foot must be turned outward and that it must make contact underneath the ball. Note also in Figure 1.9 that the toes are not pointed down but rather are nearly horizontal.

THE BACK-HEEL KICK. One other kick (probably better des-cribed as a flick) is the back-heel kick. Used for making short passes and for surprising opponents, this kick requires no-thing more than stepping over the ball and bringing the heel of the foot back hard against the ball.

Kicking exercises

One of the best ways to improve your kicking (as well as heading and trapping) is to use a wall or a wooden

Figure 1.9: Chip kick

kickboard. Most of the top soccer pros of today spent a good part of their youth practicing alone against walls, wooden fences, and any other suitable flat object.

Take some chalk and draw a small circle on any wall and use it as your target for your kicking exercises. First, try kicking a dead ball with the instep, the inside of the foot, and the outside of the foot. Then move back away from the wall so that you can practice running with the ball before you kick. You will find your kicking will not be quite so accurate when you kick a ball that is moving. This is the most important of the kicking exercises, however, since most of the kicking you will do during a soccer game will be aimed at a moving ball.

Now practice the volley and half volley by hitting the ball as it bounces off the wall. Remember to keep your toes pointed down so that your instep comes into contact with the ball.

If a friend or a teammate is available, go to a soccer field. Have him play as the goalkeeper and practice shooting the ball at the goal. Take shots with both the left and right foot, first from the right wing, then from the center of the penalty area, and finally from the left wing.

With one or more friends or teammates you can also work on your passing. Start with the inside-of-the-foot pass to each other's feet. Then try long lead passes with the instep aiming the ball far enough ahead of the receiver so that he does not have to check his stride to reach the ball.

Now form a circle and try passing the ball from one player to another without letting it go out of the circle. To make this passing practice more difficult have a teammate go into the middle of the circle and have him try to intercept your passes.

Trapping

Getting the ball is, of course, the first step in ball

control. There are many ways to stop a moving ball. The most often used are foot, thigh, chest, and head traps.

Trapping with the foot

THE INSIDE-OF-THE-FOOT TRAP. The safest and simplest method of stopping a moving ball is with the inside-of-the-foot trap, as long as you remember to relax the foot upon contact. This cushioning action can make even the fastest of balls stop dead. In Figure 1.10 the player has his foot raised a few inches off the ground to trap the ground ball. For high balls the foot is raised to the same height as the ball and moves slightly backward upon contact as in Figure 1.11.

The goal of beginners in this maneuver should be not only to learn how to trap or kill a ball with the inside of the foot but also how to slow it down so that you can move off in any direction without having to come to a dead stop. As

Figure 1.10: Inside-of-the-foot trap

Figure 1.11: High inside-of-the-foot trap

you improve, try trapping the ball and tapping it ahead of you all in one movement. Sometimes called a push-trap, this trap takes a great deal of practice to master, but once you learn it you will find your speed with the ball will be greatly improved.

THE SOLE-OF-THE-FOOT TRAP. Whenever the inside of the foot cannot be used to trap an incoming ball use the sole of the foot. The sole is useful particularly in situations like that shown in Figure 1.12, in which the player has to stretch to reach the ball. As in all other traps relax the foot upon contact. Whatever you do, do not slam your foot down onto the ball or you may well lose your balance and find yourself on the ground. And try not to raise your foot too high; if you do, the ball will probably go right under your foot.

THE INSTEP TRAP. Another way to trap high balls is to use the

Figure 1.12: Sole-of-the-foot trap   Figure 1.13: Instep trap

instep trap. The trapping foot is raised up to meet the ball, and upon contact it drops straight down to the ground. If the instep trap is executed properly the foot should take the ball with it as if it were catching it. As in the inside-of-the-foot trap, remember to let the foot give so as to produce the desired cushioning effect. If you forget and your foot is tense or it strikes at the ball, the result will most probably be that the ball will take a wild bounce or travel away from he receiver.

THE OUTSIDE-OF-THE-FOOT TRAP. This trap is generally reserved for controlling bouncing balls that land to the side of you. It is probably the most difficult of all traps. Perfect

Figure 1.14: Outside-of-the-foot trap   Figure 1.15: Thigh trap

timing is needed to ensure that the outside of the foot meets the ball just as it hits the ground. As the relaxed foot makes contact, it leans into the ball, bringing the ball to a dead stop.

Notice the arms held out wide in Figure 1.14. Balance is vital in all trapping situations. It is the outstretched arms that provide the stablizing effect.

Trapping with the body

THE THIGH TRAP. Another way to handle the dropping ball is by means of the thigh trap. Raise the leg before making contact with the ball so that the leg can be dropped toward the ground as soon as the ball hits it. If this cushioning action is performed properly the ball should drop gently to the ground, ready for your next move.

THE CHEST TRAP. Two important techniques to keep in mind for the chest trap are keeping the arms spread wide, to avoid striking the ball with the arms or hands, and relaxing the chest upon contact. Figure 1.16 shows the position of the chest for the dropping ball. Note the difference in Figure 1.17, in which the player is leaning foward to stop a ball coming straight at the player's chest.

Trapping exercises

If a friend or teammate is available,,you can kick both ground and lofted balls to each other, trapping each ball dead before returning it. Use the inside-of-the-foot, sole-of-the-foot, outside-of-the-foot, thigh, and chest traps. Vary these exercises by trying to trap the ball so it does not stop completely. This can be achieved by minimizing your cushioning action.

When there is no other player available you can use a wall to good advantage. Throw or kick the ball against the wall and trap the rebounds using all the various traps. Again,

Figure 1.16: Chest trap (when ball drops from above)

Figure 1.17: Chest trap (when ball comes straight)

vary your trapping by attempting to slow up rather than stop the ball.

Heading

Most newcomers to the game are reluctant to use the head to strike the ball. After a few practice sessions, however, you will find heading a very valuable tool and one of the more exciting plays in soccer. Surprising as it may seem, heading does not hurt, at least not when it is executed correctly. The only way to prove this is to throw up a ball and let it land on your head. . . . Yes, that probably hurt. Now throw it up and this time make the head hit the ball. . . . You didn't feel a thing, did you? The moral of this

Figure 1.18:　Preparing to head　　　Figure 1.19:　Heading

little exercise is simple: hit the ball with the head before it
hits you.

Other important rules to remember are to keep the eyes
open and on the ball and, most important, to use the
forehead—the flattest and strongest part of the skull—to
strike the ball. Figure 1.18 shows the position of the upper
torso as the ball approaches. Notice how it bends, ready to
swing into the ball for added power. In Figure 1.19 we see
that the player's neck has tightened and that the center of the
forehead is thrusting itself against the ball.

Jumping to head high balls requires accurate timing so
that the body rises to the apex of the jump just as the ball
passes over. Try taking off from one foot—you will find you
will jump higher than with a two-footed jump—and attempt
to time your effort so that your forehead is as high as the ball

Figure 1.20: Jump header

or slightly higher. Upon contact remember to thrust (or throw) your forehead against the ball.

Once you have mastered your jumping and timing try heading the ball sideways and backward, guiding it in any direction by simply twisting your neck in the desired direction.

Most forwards try to head the ball downward when attempting to score since the low ball is far more difficult for the goalkeeper to reach than one coming in at chest or head level. The lofted header is usually reserved for defenders in their own penalty area who are trying to head the ball away from a dangerous situation.

Although wearing glasses need not constitute a handicap for soccer players, care must be taken whenever a ball is headed. If you have to wear glasses I suggest that instead of heading with the forehead you try to make contact with the ball around the hairline. It may not prove to be as effective as heading with the full forehead but it will be much safer.

Trapping with the head

Sometimes you will find it more advantageous to bring the head-high ball down to the feet instead of heading it away again. The use of the head to trap the ball requires that you break one of the basic rules for heading—for you must allow the ball to hit the head so that the head gives a little upon contact. The harder the ball comes at you the more you draw the head back. This trap is undoubtedly a difficult one to master but can be a valuable addition to a player's repertoire. It is especially useful when you are attacking and unguarded and you receive a head-high pass that is too high to control with the chest. By dropping the ball to your feet you may well find yourself in a good position to shoot at the goal.

Heading exercises

A wall can be used to practice heading also. Forward, sideways, and even backwards heading can be performed easily by throwing the ball underhand against the wall. Make certain you hit the ball with your forehead regardless of which way you move your head after contact. Practice heading the ball upward into the air and also down toward the bottom of the wall.

With a teammate, practice defending and attacking from a corner kick. Remember: defenders want to move the ball up and over opponents, while attackers try to send the ball down into the goal.

Tackling

In socer, unlike in football, tackling means using the feet to take the ball away from an opponent. Pushing, body checking, and holding are all illegal in soccer; consequently, soccer tackling bears no resemblance to tackling in football. The only charge permitted in soccer is the shoulder charge. Many times a tackle is made in combination with a shoulder charge.

Figure 1.21 shows a legitimate shoulder charge. Using hands, elbows, or hips is forbidden. It must be the shoulders that meet when the players come into contact. As we will notice in Chapter 5 a shoulder charge can be fair only if the ball is within playing distance.

The block tackle

Knowing when to tackle is probably just as important as knowing how to tackle. Only practice and experience will enable you to know when to commit yourself. Rushing into the tackle wildly is seldom profitable, particularly against a player who is adept at dribbling. You should always try to get close to the ball and be well balanced when approaching for a tackle. The standing leg should be near the ball and slightly bent with the tackling foot turned outward to allow the inside of the foot to face the ball.

In Figure 1.22 the tackling foot has swung into the ball and the body is leaning over it. The whole weight of the body has now been transferred to the tackling foot giving power to the follow-through. Your foot's pressure against the ball will probably push the ball and your opponent's foot back, and quite often will cause your opponent to lose balance and fall to the ground. As long as your foot touches the ball before it touches your opponent's foot, however, your tackle is legal.

The block tackle is also used to tackle opponents on the side of you or with their backs to you. But special care must

Figure 1.21:   Shoulder charge

Figure 1.22:   Block tackle

be taken so that you come into contact with the ball first when tackling from the side or behind an opponent. Referees tend to favor the player in possession in these situations.

The sliding tackle

It is effective to employ the sliding tackle, but possession is seldom gained even when the tackle is successful. An exciting sight to see when performed correctly, the sliding tackle is normally used only when a block tackle is not possible, such as when the ball is too far away. The reason for its limited use is that not only is possession unlikely but, more important, the tackler is usually left stranded on the ground and momentarily out of the game.

Figure 1.23 shows the tackling foot beginning its swing with the standing leg bending, always closest to the ball.

In Figure 1.24 the tackle has been made and we can see that the player's left arm is breaking his fall as his right foot kicks the ball away.

Tackling exercises

To tackle successfully you must go in with absolute determination to win the ball. Consequently, practicing full-blooded tackles with a teammate can be risky, since it is in tackling that most soccer injuries occur. How to practice tackling without inadvertently injuring members of the team has always been a problem for coaches. I suggest you attempt to improve your basic technique in tackling and forget about developing a more powerful tackle during your practice sessions. Here are a few exercises that should help you improve your skill with a minimum risk of inflicting accidental injuries.

1. Have a teammate stand with the ball at his foot. Tackle firmly with your right foot so that most of the inside of the foot comes into contact with the ball. To avoid injury, your teammate should offer little resistance and permit his

Figure 1.23:   Swinging into the slide tackle

Figure 1.24:   Slide tackle

foot to be pushed back by yours. Repeat this exercise with the left foot.

2. Now have your teammate take the ball about six to eight yards away from you and start dribbling the ball slowly toward you. When he is within playing distance (two or three yards away) you must step forward with your left foot and tackle with your right. Again he should offer little resistance, allowing you to practice without danger of injury. Repeat this exercise with the left foot.

3. Have your teammate dribble the ball along the touchline and practice tackling from the side and slide tackling.

In all of the above exercises you should exchange roles with your teammate to give him the opportunity to practice his tackling.

4. In addition to improving your tackling techniques you must work on improving your timing. Knowing just when to make the tackle is often more important than knowing how. A good exercise to sharpen this skill is trying to take the ball away from two teammates who must keep the ball inside a small circle.

Dribbling

Probably the most difficult of all individual skills to perfect, dribbling is also the most exciting. Moving past opponents with the ball at the player's feet, feinting, twisting, and turning while all the time keeping the ball under close control is one of soccer's great delights for both player and spectator alike.

Dribbling well requires that the ball be maneuvered with gentle taps rather than with hefty kicks, using the inside and the outside of the feet. You will also have to learn how far to push the ball ahead of you so that it is always under your control. A good rule of thumb is this: the faster you run the farther ahead of you the ball should be kicked. You

Figure 1.25: Dribbling with the inside of the foot

Figure 1.26: Dribbling with the outside of the foot

should also run quickly with short strides so that you can change directions without losing your balance.

In Figure 1.25 the player is leaning over the ball as he dribbles, and he comes down gently on the balls of his feet. Notice that his right foot is turned outward, enabling him to use the part of the inside of the foot alongside his big toe for gentle contact.

In Figure 1.26 it is the outside of the foot—the toe area again—that is controlling the ball.

Dribbling tricks

Once you have learned how to move the ball from foot to foot while on the run you are ready for some tricks. All dribbling tricks rely upon a change of pace and use the feet and body to confuse opponents.

The most common trick, the body feint, is shown in Figure 1.27. Here the player has leaned his body toward the left and then proceeded to use the outside of his right foot to move the ball to the right. As in all dribbling tricks, once you are past your opponent it is essential that you accelerate

Figure 1.27: Body feint

Figure 1.28:   Leg-over-ball trick

quickly; otherwise he will catch up with you and once more obstruct your progress.

Stepping on the ball with the sole of the foot to stop it suddenly is another convenient way to trick your opponent, especially if you are running at top speed.

Figure 1.28 shows the leg-over-the-ball trick in which the leg goes over and across the ball before the dribbler taps it with the same foot in the opposite direction.

Another simple trick is to push the ball through your opponent's legs if he comes at you with them far apart.

You will probably learn many dribbling tricks as you progress in soccer. Try to remember that dribbling should be undertaken only when a suitable pass or shot is not possible. Although a good dribbler can be a great asset to a team, far too many players overuse the dribble, holding on to the ball when a quick pass might well prove fruitful.

Screening

A vital part of the dribbling process is screening the ball

Figure 1.29:   Screening

from opponents. As Figure 1.29 shows, the body is placed between the ball and the opponent, making it more difficult for the opponent to get near it. Notice also that the dribbler is steering the ball with the foot farthest away from his opponent.

Running with the ball

Although at first it may seem the same as dribbling, running with the ball is quite different. When there is ample space in which to run without having to beat an opponent, a different style of running is required from dribbling. It is much faster and more direct than the tap-tapping, stop-and-go movements of dribbling.

Figure 1.30:   Running with the ball

To move the ball at top speed the player turns his toes inward so that the outside of the foot comes into contact with the ball as the foot touches the ground. The ball is also kicked farther ahead than in dribbling since the faster you run the longer your stride should be.

Dribbling exercises

The most basic exercise and probably the most valuable one for beginners is simply standing with the ball at the feet, gently nudging it from one foot to the other. As you jump lightly from foot to foot use the big toe area of the inside of the foot to hit the ball each time a foot touches the ground. The idea of this exercise is to keep the ball between the feet without moving from your stationary position. As you get the feel of the ball you can vary this exercise by deliberately moving the ball forward and then backward at a slow jogging pace.

Now speed up your jogging pace and begin to use not only the toe area of the inside of the foot to control the ball but the outside of the foot too. Run for approximately 20 yards before stepping on the ball gently with the sole of the foot; then dribble in the reverse direction.

Another good exercise is dribbling in between stakes or flags. Place your obstacles about six feet from each other so that you must keep the ball under tight control to pass through without touching them. Make certain that you use both feet to manipulate the ball.

A very useful skill that will help your dribbling is juggling. Although it should not be used during the heat of a game it is a marvelous tool for improving your overall ball control, warming up for a game, and instilling self-confidence.

Keeping the ball off the ground either with the feet, with the thighs, with the chest, or with the head is what juggling is all about. The difficult part of juggling is the very first step—getting the dead ball off the ground with the foot so that is can then be manipulated with some other part of the body. To accomplish this, place the sole of your foot on the ball. Shift your weight onto your nonkicking foot. Roll the ball backward toward you with your kicking foot. Then, just as soon as you have it rolling, remove your foot and quickly place it under the ball. Flick the ball up by bending your big toe upwards. Once it is off the ground you can use either foot to move it up to any height so that the thighs, chest, head, and even the top of the shoulders can be brought into play. Try to keep the ball off the ground for ten touches.

Whenever you have the opportunity you should also practice running with the ball. Most beginners neglect to do this, concentrating instead on dribbling.

A good running exercise is running at a jogging pace

while trying to keep the ball along any one of the chalk lines on a soccer field, such as the goal line, the halfway line, or the touchline. Remember, of course, to keep the toes pointed inward as the foot strikes the ball. Once you find you are able to keep the ball near or on the line try speeding up your pace until you are running at a sprint.

Photo 3:   Derek Trevis (18) of Las Vegas and Leroy DeLeon of San Jose tussle for the ball while being watched by Wolfgang Suhnholz.

32

2

The goalkeeper

Once thought of solely as the last line of defense, the goalkeeper in modern soccer has also become an important part of offensive soccer. Today every time he gains possession of the ball he is expected to start off an attacking move. A quick throw to a nearby teammate or a long kick across the halfway line to an unmarked (unguarded) forward can very well begin a counterattack resulting in a goal.

This recent tactical shift in the use of the goalkeeper has in no way diminished his defensive duties. No matter how accurate his distribution, be it by throwing or kicking, he will be unsuccessful unless he can stop the opposition from scoring.

To succeed as a goalkeeper there are three essential prerequisites. The first is agility—for goalies spend most of their active moments during a game diving and jumping in pursuit of the ever-moving ball. The second is the ability to catch well—one reason why so many basketball players make such splendid goalkeepers. The third important quality all

33

goalies must possess is courage—the type of fearlessness that sends them flying across crowded goalmouths or diving at the feet of an onrushing opponent.

If you are agile, a good catcher, and courageous and you want to become a goalkeeper the first step in your apprenticeship should be learning the three basic K's:

Keep your body behind the ball whenever possible.
Keep your eyes on the ball at all times.
Keep alert (even when the ball is in your opponent's half of the field).

Defense

Catching the ball

GROUND BALLS. There are two ways to handle incoming balls at ground level. One such method is seen in Figure 2.2: the goalkeeper is standing with the legs together, bending from the waist to collect the ball. Notice that the hands are behind the ball with the fingers pointing down.

For harder shots it is better to go down on one knee as in Figure 2.3. After performing either the standing or the kneeling save, make certain you bring the ball up to the chest for added protection in case of a collision with another player.

WAIST-HIGH AND CHEST-HIGH BALLS. Again we see the goalkeeper using both hands in Figure 2.4. With the chest as a backup barrier it is clear that the ball will not go by the goalie even if he fails to make a clean catch.

HIGH BALLS. When attempting to save a high ball always get the hands behind the ball with the fingers pointing upward. Try to time your save so that you catch the ball at the highest point of your jump with the arms fully stretched above the head. Once you have caught the ball, bring it down to your chest.

Figure 2.2:   Incoming ball at ground level

Figure 2.3:   Down on one knee

Figure 2.4:   Using both hands on chest-high ball

Figure 2.5:   Hands behind a high ball

Punching and deflecting

Sometimes it is extemely risky to attempt a clean catch. A slippery ball on a wet day, a crowed goalmouth, or a ball cleverly sent spinning away from the goalmouth are sufficient reasons for even the best of goalies to opt for a punch or deflection.

Figure 2.6 shows a two-handed punch—always preferable to a one-handed attempt. The ball should be punched back in the direction from which it came, thus reducing the chance that the ball may be deflected. And whatever you do, never hit halfheartedly. The farther away from your goal you send the ball the better it will be for your defense.

Figure 2.6: Two-handed punch

Figure 2.7: Deflect-
ing ball over crossbar

Deflecting or tipping a ball over the crossbar is accomp-
lished by using the palms of the hands or the fingers. Do not
use the backs of the hands since there is always the likelihood
that the ball could bounce off your knuckles back into the
goalmouth, or even worse, into your goal.

Diving

Once you have learned to stop balls that come directly
at you it is time to move on to the more difficult balls that
arrive five feet or more away from you. Diving sideways
through the air is, of course, the only way of saving the shot
that is not within arm's reach.

When well executed, the diving save is exciting action
for both the goalkeeper and the fans. The legs push off

Figure 2.8: Diving save

thrusting the body in the direction of the ball. As Figure 2.8 indicates, the goalkeeper flings his body sideways so that it is possible for him to keep his eyes on the ball as well as have his body available for a shield just in case of an overdive or a swerve in the ball's flight. When falling, the goalie lands on his forearms and side and quickly brings the ball to his chest for protection.

Quite often a shot will be too difficult for you to catch with a dive, either too far away for a two-handed attempt, or hit too hard. In these cases you should dive and try to punch the ball out of danger or deflect it around the post.

Anticipation and positioning

Although diving is a spectacular sight, the top professional goalies try to minimize the need for it by learning correct positioning and refining their intuitive anticipatory senses. Watch one of the top NASL golies like Tony Chursky of Seattle, Gordon Banks of Fort Lauderdale, Bob Rigby of Los Angeles, or Merv Cawston of Chicago and you will notice that most incoming balls seem to have been shot right at them. And, indeed, most of the time they are, for with skill in anticipation and positioning, each has placed himself in a direct line between the kicker and the goal. For example, if an opponent is approaching from your left then you must move toward your left goalpost. The opposite would, of course, apply if the attack were coming from the right side. Action in front of the center of the goalmouth would necessitate your moving back to the point midway between the two goalposts.

For corner kicks you should always stand by the far post (the post farthest away from the ball). Here again, it is all a matter of common sense, since it is much easier to run forward when the ball falls short of the far post than to run backward when the ball goes over your head, as it may well do if you stand by the near post. In addition, the goalie has the benefit of seeing all that is happening around the goalmouth if he stays by the far post.

Many times you will have to move off your goal line to make a save, especially to cut off any high ball that comes inside your goal area, that 20 by 6-yard box immediately in front of the goal. You must be in complete command of the goal area and be prepared to yell to your teammates, "Goalie's ball!" anytime they are in the way.

A good rule of thumb that will improve your anticipation skill is always to move off your goal line whenever an opponent has beaten your defense and is advancing toward the goal unchallenged. By moving off your line you are able to reduce the amount of goal he can shoot at. As Figure 2.9 indicates, the farther you advance the harder it becomes for him to fire a shot that can avoid you. This is called narrowing the angle and is one of the most important concepts in soccer for any goalkeeper.

When narrowing the angle, keep in mind that the

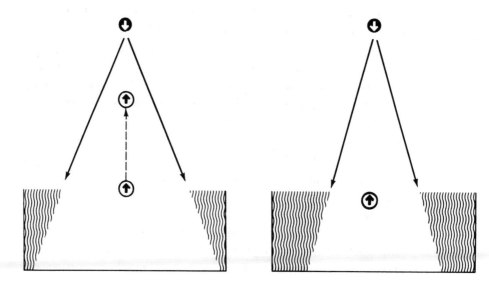

Figure 2.9: Narrowing the angle

farther you advance the greater the opportunity for the opponent to lob or chip the ball over your head. In addition, a forward may attempt to dribble the ball around you if you attempt to dive at his feet. In either situation, anticipating your opponent's next move is the vital key. As you progress in soccer you will get to know all about your opponents' strengths, weaknesses, and favorite tricks.

Penalty kicks

Knowing something about your opponents can be of immeasurable value whenever a penalty kick is awarded against your team. Because the penalty spot is only 12 yards away from the goal, the goalie should have little hope of saving a penalty kick. Yet many top goalies have a high percentage of successful saves. They achieve this by studying how opponents usually take penalties—which side of the goal they usually aim for, whether they favor low or high shots, and whether they prefer hard drives or gentle spins.

Offense

As soon as a goalkeeper gets possession of the ball he becomes an attacker. There are three times a goalkeeper gets possession of the ball: when the ball goes over the goal line for a goal kick, when he makes a save, and when a teammate passes the ball back to him.

Kicking

It is the goalie who usually takes the goal kick. (Sometimes a teammate with a powerful kick might be called upon to do it.) The most popular forms of goal kicks are the long, lofted instep kick, which many goalies can kick far over the halfway line; the short instep kick; and the inside-of-the-foot kick to a teammate positioned just outside the penalty area.

A short kick is undoubtedly better for retaining possession. Quite often, however, there are no unmarked teammates available to receive a short pass, and it is unwise, indeed it is foolhardy, to kick the ball just outside your penalty area when there are opponents nearby. For this reason the long kick is still used extensively.

Unlike in the dead ball situation, in the goal kick once the goalie gets the live ball in his hands he has the further choice of either kicking or throwing. If he decides to kick he will probably punt the ball on the volley. The punt goes farther than any form of kick. The leg is brought back for a full swing and the ball is hit squarely on the instep, as shown in Figure 2.10. The follow-through is higher than for the instep kick.

Throwing

Punts are commonly used when there are no unguarded teammates available nearby to accept a short pass from the goalie. But the modern goalie's best use of the ball is to throw it to the feet of a teammate, thus ensuring that his

Figure 2.10:   Punt

own team will retain it. The three methods of throwing are the bowling, the javelin, and the overarm throw.

The bowling throw is usually directed to a teammate who is close by, since it is the weakest of all the throws. Arriving as it does on the ground, the bowling throw is favored by the outfield players since they do not have to concern themselves with controlling a high or bouncing ball.

The javelin throw is also very accurate but the ball is usually airborne when it is received. As Figure 2.12 shows, the goalie's hand is behind the ball and the arm is bent.

The overarm throw is used for long throws. Some goalies can throw the ball farther than they can kick. The back swing begins behind the waist with the non-throwing arm held out for balance. The important point to remember

Figure 2.11: Bowling throw

in the overarm throw is keeping the throwing arm straight and above the head when the ball is released.

Goalkeeping exercises

As a goalkeeper your best practice sessions will be, of course, with at least one other teammate. If someone is available you can go through all the various saves: catching, punching, deflecting, and even coming off your line and cutting down the angle in a one-on-one situation. In addition, try to get a teammate to stand by the goal and pressure you while another teammate kicks corner kicks high into the goalmouth.

43

Figure 2.12:   Javelin throw   Figure 2.13:   Overarm throw

But even alone the goalkeeper can perform some useful exercises. Here are a few:

1. Stand about five yards from a wall and throw or kick the ball against it, saving the rebound. Adjust your throw or kick so that the ball comes at you at varying heights. Now try punching and deflecting the rebounds.

2. Stand 15 to 20 yards away from the wall and practice kicking with the instep. Even though a goalkeeper tries to get height into his long goal kicks, unless you have a very high wall you will have to keep the ball low, so make certain your body is over it when you kick. Make the appropriate type of save on each rebound. For obvious reasons, it is unwise to practice diving when on a cement or other hard surface.

3. One other good exercise for goalkeepers with nothing but a low wall to work with is to combine practicing the javelin throw, bowling throw, and even the overarm throw with picking up the ball on the rebounds. Do this in both the standing position, with the knees slightly bent, and the kneeling position, with one knee on the ground.

Photo 4: George Davies of San Jose heads the ball despite the close marking by Mick Hoban of Portland. (Photo by Michael Rapping)

3

The team in action

After a short period of apprenticeship while you learn the skills, you probably will be invited to play for a team. One of the first things you will realize after joining a team is that there is much more to soccer than acquiring a few or even all of the skills.

As a member of a team you will have the responsibility of learning about tactical formations, positional play, support, space, and many other concepts that will enable your team to utilize all the skills you have to offer.

Team formations

In discussions of team formations the goalkeeper is always omitted, since his position remains constant. The other ten players (often called outfield players) are divided into defenders, midfielders, and forwards. Just how many of each is decided by the team's coach, but generally in modern soccer it is considered risky to have fewer than four defend-

ers. The most popular of present-day team formations—
reading from goal to center field—are 4-2-4 (four defenders,
two midfielders, and four forwards), 4-3-3 (four defenders,
three midfielders, and three forwards), and 4-4-2 (four defenders, four midfielders, and two forwards).

The 4-2-4 formation

Of the three formations 4-2-4 is the most offensive in
nature, but a tremendous amount of midfield responsibility
falls upon the two midfielders. In modern soccer it is the
midfield that is the key to success. All too often the two
midfielders of 4-2-4 systems are not strong enough to handle
all the duties of linking the defense with the offense.

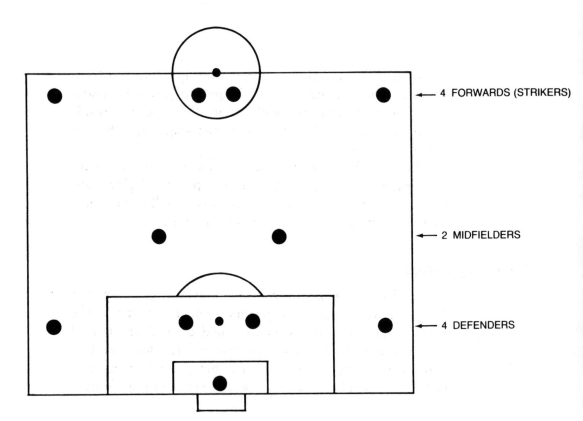

Figure 3.2:   4-2-4 Formation

The 4-3-3 formation

It was because of the strain on the two midfielders that an additional midfielder was added in the early 1960s; thus the 4-3-3 system was introduced. (See Figure 3.3.) Although one player was taken away from the forward line, there has not been a noticeable diminution in goal scoring when 4-3-3 has been played with attack-conscious midfielders. Indeed, the gap left by the missing forward is filled not only by midfielders but also by defenders, who move up into an attack position. This is called overlapping and is a feature of 4-3-3 play. Notice in Figure 3.4 how the outside defender has moved ahead of his three forwards into the space that would belong in a 4-2-4 system to the right winger (a forward who plays along the touchlines).

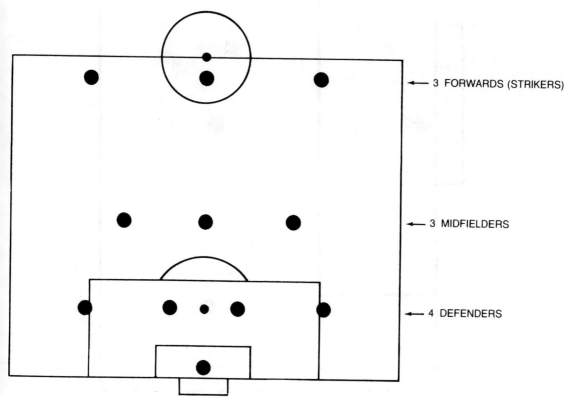

Figure 3.3: 4-3-3 Formation

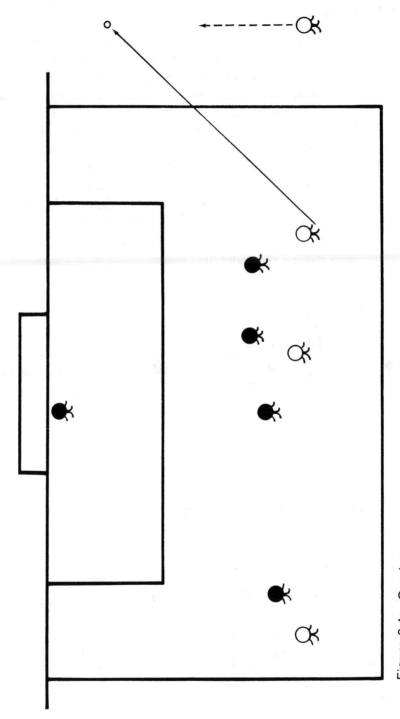

Figure 3.4: Overlap

The 4-4-2 formation

The 4-4-2 system is definitely a defensive formation with emphasis on maintaining preponderance in the midfield. The offensive strategy is based upon quick breakaways, with the two lone forwards attempting to keep possession of the ball until the midfielders arrive to help.

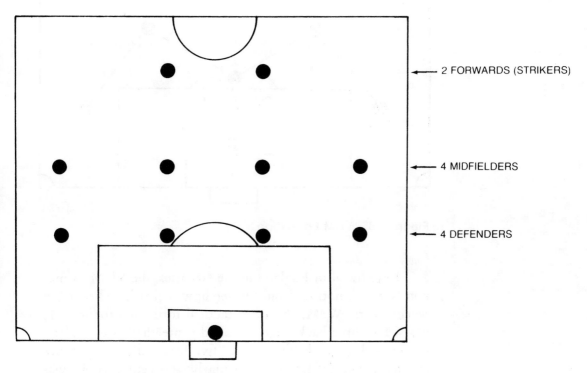

Figure 3.5: 4-4-2 Formation

The W-M formation

There are many other ways to utilize the ten out-fielders. Some teams use a "sweeper" or a "cleanup" player in a 1-3-3-3 lineup, and a few more conservative teams field a 1-4-4-1, while there are a few teams that still stick to the old W-M formation of the pre-1960s.

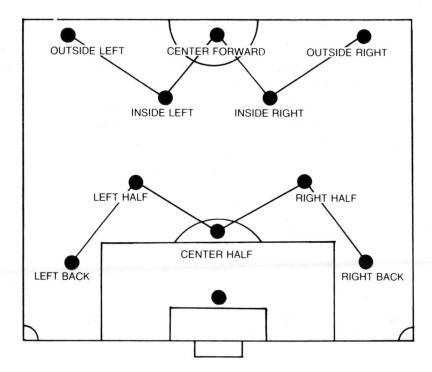

Figure 3.6:   W-M Formation

Introduced in England in the twenties, the W-M formation is worth noting if only to see how soccer has changed in
recent years. W-M, the basic tactical formation for over 40
years, has three backs (the so-called center half was in fact a
center back), two halfbacks, and five forwards. The pressure
on the three defenders, particularly the center back, was
relieved in the late fifties when the Brazilians devised the
concept of using two center backs, the 4-2-4 system.

Team positions

The nearly complete changeover to the modern team
formations has brought with it new names for some of the
team positions. "Halfbacks" are now "midfielders," "center
forwards" are now "strikers," and "center half" has disap-

peared from soccer language to be replaced by "center back."

Not only the terminology for positions has changed since the 1950s, but the style of play also has changed. Today defenders are no longer simply the toughest tacklers on the team who are also capable of booting long balls out of dangerous situations. Rather, like everyone else on the team, they must be adept at offensive as well as defensive functions. Whenever they gain possession of the ball, by either tackling or intercepting, they are expected to pass it effectively or move upfield quickly with it.

The midfielders are the unselfish coordinators and work-horses of the team. They must plot attacking movements from the midfield area in addition to helping out in both the defense and the attack. They do more running than anyone else on the team and need to be as proficient at tackling as any defender when possession is lost, and as creative and goal-hungry as any forward when they have the ball.

The job of a forward or striker is, of course, to score goals. In modern soccer, especially in top-class soccer, it is becoming increasingly difficult to get the ball into the back of the net. Because of the modern trend toward packed defenses, with five, six, and sometimes seven defenders in the penalty area, the opportunity to score goals unimpeded is rare. A forward or striker, therefore, must be able to play the ball skillfully even when surrounded by two or more opponents. Exceptional ball control, the ability to screen the ball, courage, and speedy acceleration—these are the prerequisites for making one's mark as a forward or striker.

If a team is using wingers (forwards who play along the touchlines), there probably will be a great many high balls coming across for the central strikers to head. This means the latter players must be adept at heading under great pressure. On the other hand, if the team's usual approach to goal is carried out along the ground, the strikers must be especially capable of receiving the ball while facing their own goal and turning with it despite the close marking of the opposing defenders.

Offensive soccer

Another change brought about in modern soccer in the last two decades has been the general shift to possession soccer. This means maintaining possession by passing the ball between teammates even if it means they must advance circuitously, moving the ball backward and laterally as well as forward until a reasonable goal-scoring opportunity arises. Players no longer hit many long passes 40 or 50 yards upfield with the hope that marked teammates would somehow manage to get to them before the opposing defenders would. Such passes are considered by modern coaches to be "high risk" balls. This is not to imply that coaches no longer favor the "long ball" or long pass, but only that it is more wisely used at such times as when the intended receiver is unmarked, or when he can run into an open space to meet the ball.

Space

Creating space is the most important element is offensive soccer. There are two ways of achieving space: (1) sending the ball to an unmarked teammate, and (2) creating space where none exists. Figures 3.7 and 3.8 show examples of both.

Because creating space is so vital to a team's performance it is essential that the players without the ball run to good positions to receive the ball. In soccer this is called running off the ball, a continuous movement of players in support of the teammate with the ball. It entails a tremendous amount of running and is one reason why you must be absolutely fit to play soccer.

Passing

Most coaches, at least in adult soccer, prefer a particular style when it comes to passing. Some favor the short pass;

54

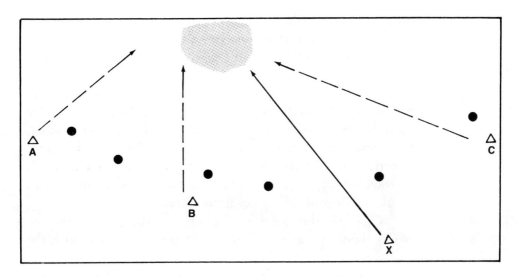

Figure 3.7:   Existing space

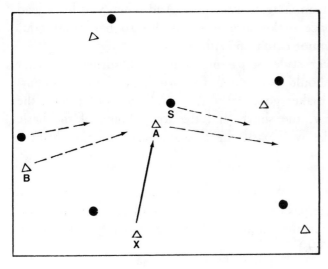

Figure 3.8:   Creating space

others the long; and many stress a combination in which the long is used only for swift counterattacks.

Both the short and the long passes have advantages and disadvantages. Even the beginner will notice how much easier it is to maintain possession with short passes although progress up the field will not be rapid. Similarly, any novice will soon discover that long passes are the quickest way to cover territory while yielding more time to the opposition to intercept the ball.

Another aspect of a team's passing style is whether the ball is played mainly on the ground or in the air. Generally most coaches prefer to see the ball passed along the ground, but there are occasions when the high ball can be more effective than the low. A good example is when a defender is surrounded by opponents and a ground pass, if attempted, would in all probability be intercepted.

Coaches also have set policies relating to where the passes should be aimed. Some want their players to kick the ball directly to the feet of teammates. Others want their players to kick the ball a yard or two ahead. I suggest you always aim for the feet unless you are attempting a "lead pass" for a teammate to run onto. And when you hit a lead pass into space make sure it is not hit so hard that your teammate cannot catch up with it.

Whatever style of passing is utilized, surprise is what your team should be aiming for. To keep your opponents guessing, it makes good sense to use all types of passes, the high, the low, the short, and the long. Some of the basic passes are the wall pass, the scissors pass, and the through pass.

THE WALL PASS. With one player acting as the wall and another as the passer and runner, the wall pass (or give-and-go) is probably the simplest way to get around an opponent. (See Figure 3.9.)

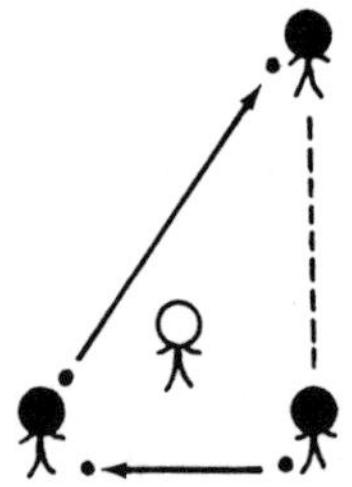

Figure 3.9: Wall pass

THE SCISSORS PASS. An effective way to confuse an opponent is to have two teammates, one with the ball, run across each other's path. Until they meet, the opponent has no way of

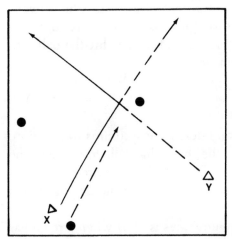

Figure 3.10: Scissors pass

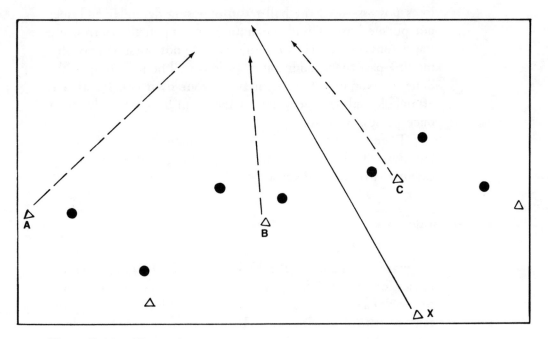

Figure 3.11: Through pass

knowing which one will emerge with the ball. In Figure 3.10, X has given the ball to Y but continues to run as if he still has possession.

THE THROUGH PASS. The most potent of all passes but always difficult to execute, the through pass is best left to teams having speedy strikers. In Figure 3.11, X has hit the ball into space for A, B, or C to run onto.

Defensive soccer

The ultimate aim of any defensive system is to get more defending players nearer the ball than players from the attacking team. To achieve this ideal situation midfielders and even forwards must drop back to help the defense when possession is lost.

Just as support of all teammates is vital when a team has possession, so it is also when the ball is lost. If a forward loses possession of the ball to an opposing defender and does not pursue him, it will mean an extra opponent confronting the defense. Similarly, if midfielders do not pursue opponents moving past them, additional burdens will be placed upon the defense. Numerical superiority in your own penalty area is attainable only if everyone on the team becomes a defender once possession is lost.

Defense systems include man–to–man, zone, and a combination of the two. Effective pivoting and marking are essential to a good defense.

Man-to-man defense

In this defensive system each opponent is closely marked or guarded whenever the ball crosses the halfway line and possession is lost. The purpose behind this system is not only to block each forward's approach to goal but, just as important, also to intercept passes before the forwards are able to receive them. If your defenders are top players this defensive

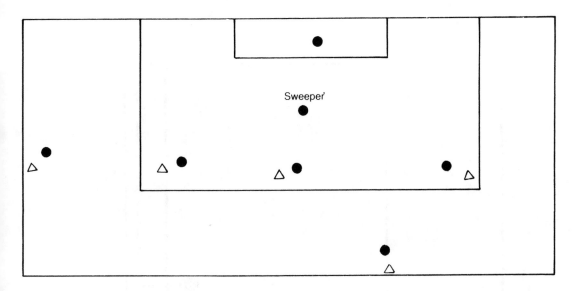

Figure 3.12:   Man-to-man defense with a sweeper

system will be hard to pierce. Unfortunately, if there is a weak link and a defender is beaten, a gap will open up in the defense.

To solve this deficiency many teams using the man-to-man also employ a defender as a "sweeper" behind the defensive wall. His job is to cut off any opponent breaking through. Figure 3.12 shows a man-to-man defense with each defender marking an opponent except the sweeper, who is free to roam to block any opponent who penetrates the defensive line.

Zone defense

A much more flexible system is the zone or zonal defense. As Figure 3.13 shows, each defender has a certain area to guard in his team's own half of the field. Notice how X is picked up by a new defender as he moves across in front of each defender's portion of the penalty area.

Like the man-to-man defense, this system also has its drawback, namely, that opponents are afforded great

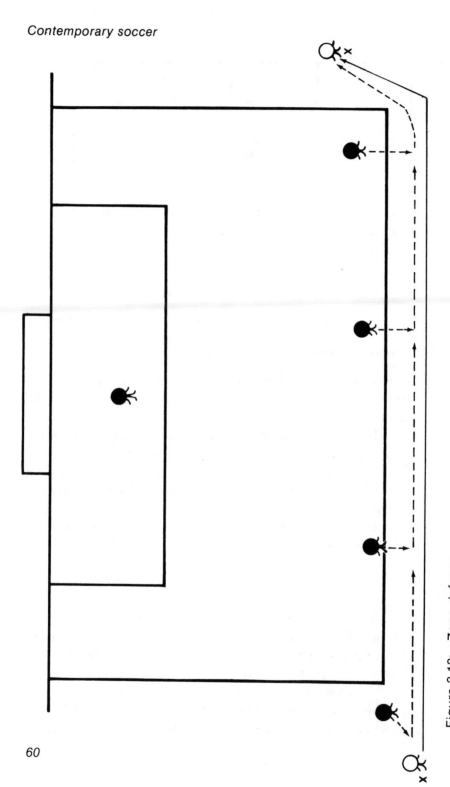

Figure 3.13: Zone defense

amounts of space. Because of this, most zonal defenses use a midfielder to patrol in front of the defense. Acting very much like the sweeper in the man-to-man setup, the midfielder (often called a free man) tries to tackle any opponent coming toward the defense. By doing so the free man is able to harass the approaching opponent and deprive him of free space.

In recent years the deficiencies of both the man-to-man and the zonal have been reduced considerably by combining the two. The defense that has emerged is a zonal when the ball is in the opponents' half and a man-to-man when the opponents bring the ball over the halfway line and advance close to the penalty area.

Pivot system

Essential to any effective defensive system is good covering by one's teammates. Whenever a defender is "beaten" another must move over to take on the advancing opponent, and a third defender in turn has to move into the spot the second defender has just vacated. This cycle of defenders covering for each other is called the pivot system.

Figure 3.14 is a good example of how each defender has to concern himself not only with the nearest opponent but also with the opponent being marked by his closest teammate. Notice how X, who has been beaten by O, is running back to get into another good defensive position.

Marking

When marking or guarding always try to position yourself between your opponent and your goal. And like everything else in soccer keep your eyes on the ball; do not watch your opponent's feet or legs. When you decide to tackle be quite certain that you are in a good position to win the ball. Often it pays just to run alongside your opponent and wait

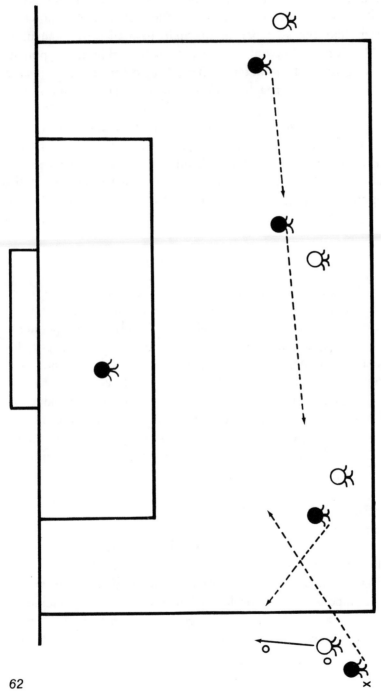

Figure 3.14:   Pivot system

for him to make a mistake before going in for the tackle. If the ball is loose (running free) then by all means commit yourself wholeheartedly; but once your opponent has the ball under control be careful. A wild rush will probably result in your opponent's flicking the ball around you and continuing on his way.

Photo 5: Los Angeles' Bob McAlinden and Bruce Twamley of the Cosmos (22) attempt to control a loose ball. (Photo by Oto Maxmilian)

4

Restarts

Whenever the referee blows his whistle to stop play, the ball is dead—whether it has gone out of play over the touchlines or the goal lines, or whether the game has been stopped for an infringement of the laws or for an injury. The game is restarted after the ball goes out of play with either a throw-in, a goal kick, or a corner kick. The game is restarted after other stopped play with either a free kick or a drop ball. In addition, a kickoff is used to start or restart play at the beginning of the half or after a goal is scored.

We have already discussed goal kicks in Chapter 2. The other restarts are discussed here.

The throw-in

The throw-in is awarded to the team opposing the one whose player last touched the ball before it crossed the touchlines. A player throws the ball from the place where the ball went over the line.

Despite the simplicity of the throw-in procedure, the throw-in is often performed incorrectly—even by professionals. The rules state that the player must throw the ball with both hands over the head; that the ball must be released while it is over the head; and that both of the thrower's feet must be on the ground. (See Figure 4.2) Many beginners, however, release the ball when it has already passed over the

Figure 4.2: Throw-in

head and is level with the chest. All too many lift one or both feet when throwing.

Like any other restart the throw-in can be a valuable advantage if performed with accuracy and vision. Ideally the ball should be thrown directly to a teammate's feet so that he can either race off with it or pass it back to you. A throw to your teammate's head can also be effective, particularly if he can direct it back to you or to another teammate. Throwing into an empty space can also be fruitful providing your teammate expects it. Figure 4.3 gives a typical preplanned throw-in with both the thrower and receiver knowing what to expect.

Some teams have players capable of making a "long throw" of up to 40 or 45 yards. A long throw near your opponent's penalty area becomes more like a free kick and can be a splendid weapon for any offensive team.

Kickoff

There are three situations in soccer in which kickoffs occur:

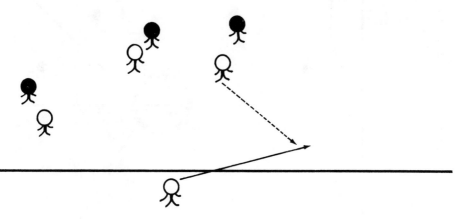

Figure 4.3: Throwing to space

1. At the beginning of the game (the kick is taken by the team which having won the toss of the coin elects to kick off, or by the opposing team if the winner of the toss decides it would rather have the choice of ends of the field)

2. At the beginning of the second half (the kick is taken by the team which did not kick off at the beginning of the game)

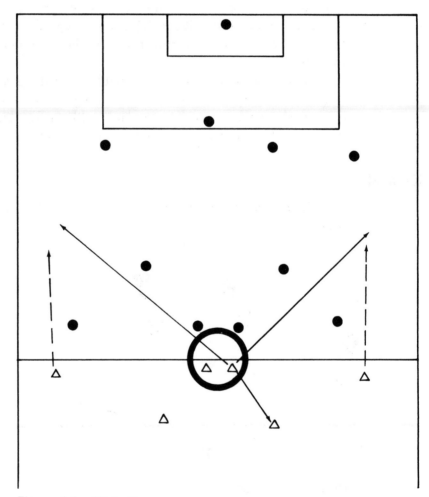

Figure 4.4:   Kickoff

3. After a goal is scored (the team conceding the goal kicks off)

The object of the kickoff in soccer differs from that in football, for in soccer the aim is to retain possession. Generally there are three ways to exploit a kickoff. All are shown in Figure 4.4, and all are based upon the concept of maintaining possession until a sufficient number of teammates can move over into the opponent's half.

The free kick

Except for the penalty kick, which is taken from the penalty spot, all free kicks are taken from the precise place where the infringement occurs.

As we noted in the Introduction, there are two types of free kicks, the direct for the nine more serious types of violations and the indirect for six lesser fouls. Either one presents a goal-scoring opportunity when awarded near or in the penalty area since most adult and many junior soccer players can hit a ball into the goal with power and accuracy from 20 or 25 yards.

Because of the imminent danger all free kicks near the goal are met by a human wall of defenders hoping to protect a part of the goal and thereby leave the goalie less area to cover. In addition, all offensive players are closely guarded by the rest of the team not being used in the four- or five-player wall.

Even the indirect free kick can create serious problems for a defense despite the fact that a goal cannot be scored directly from the kick (unless it is touched or played by someone other than the kicker). The rule that keeps defenders ten yards away from the ball at all free kicks until the ball is kicked gives an extra advantage to the team taking an indirect free kick. If the kicker and a teammate stand inches from each other the ball can be passed to and shot by the teammate before the defenders can reach it.

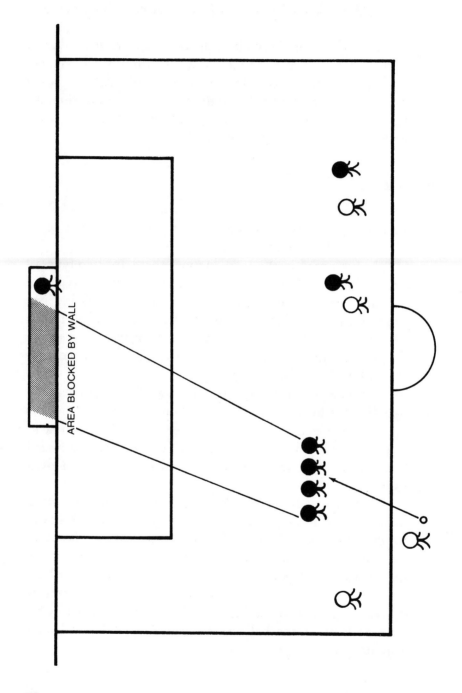

AREA BLOCKED BY WALL

Figure 4.5:   A defensive wall

Figure 4.5 shows a typical wall confronting the offensive team during an indirect free kick. Notice the goalie has entrusted to his wall the right side of the goal (as he faces the field).

Although the combination of the wall and the goalie may give the impression of forming an impregnable defense, many goals are scored from free kicks. Figure 4.6 shows some of the ways the wall can be bypassed, assuming, of course,

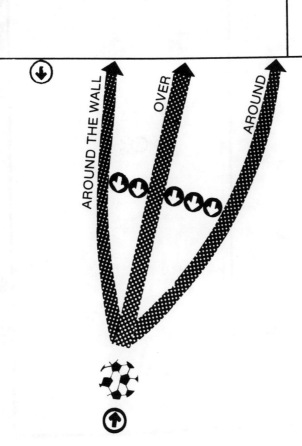

Figure 4.6: Beating the wall

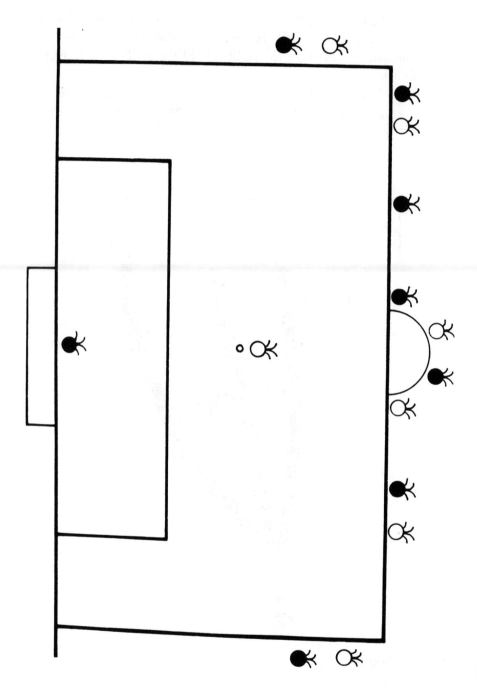

Figure 4.7:   Penalty kick

you have players on your team who can chip, curve, or "bend" the ball. Certainly many pro players have the ability to hit the ball accurately with the instep or the outside of the foot in order to impart tremendous spin to it. George Best of Los Angeles and Rodney Marsh of Tampa are two who can make the ball swerve violently over and around any defensive wall.

The penalty kick

Any direct free kick awarded to the offensive team in the defender's penalty area automatically becomes a penalty kick. One player is chosen by his team to take penalties whenever the team is fortunate enough to have them awarded. Anytime you attempt a penalty kick, aim for the corner of the goal. It is difficult not to score from a penalty unless you miskick or the goalie makes an incredible save. The usual reason for failure is that players try to hit the ball too hard, thereby trading a certain amount of accuracy for power.

The corner kick

The corner kick is awarded to the offensive team whenever the ball was last touched by the defensive team before it crossed the goal line. It is kicked from within the one-yard corner kick arc.

Corner kicks can be taken in either of two basic ways: the player can kick a high ball into the goalmouth, or he can kick a short ball to a teammate near the corner arc.

The high ball is employed usually when the offensive team possesses one or more players who are skilled at heading, particularly when they are tall and capable of rising high above the opposition. If this type of corner kick is used, it is important that the ball be floated across the goalmouth far enough from the goal to deter the goalkeeper from coming out of intercept it. In Figure 4.8 the shaded area on either side of the goal is where the ball should be kicked.

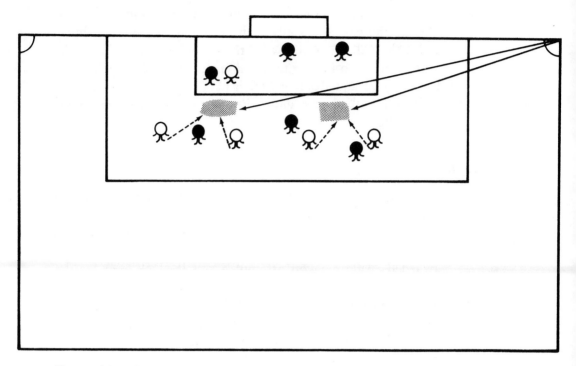

Figure 4.8:   Corner kick

To get the ball to the desired area a short corner kick can be curved into or away from the goalmouth. To hit an outswinger from the right corner arc (or from the right wing) the ball is hit with the right foot. For an inswinger the left foot is used. From the other corner arc (or the left wing) the opposite feet are used: the left for an outswinger and the right for an inswinger.

Since all opponents must be ten yards away when a corner kick is taken, a short corner kick to a teammate standing alongside can be very useful. Even if an opponent rushes at the receiver the two teammates together should be able to bypass him and advance toward the goal. And if the offensive player is confronted by other defenders he still will be in a closer and probably better position to pass the ball into the goalmouth than when the corner kick was originally taken.

The drop ball

The drop ball is a device used by the referee to restart the game after play has been halted for something other than an infringement of the laws—a serious injury, for example. The ball is dropped by the referee at the place where the ball was being played when the game was halted. Two players, one from each team, stand facing each other and the referee drops the ball between them. The ball is in play as soon as it touches the ground. The drop ball is not a very significant event unless it is in the penalty area—when a lucky touch of the ball might send it to a striker in a good scoring position.

Photo 6:   American women are in the forefront of soccer's rapid growth.

5

Understanding the rules

The 17 rules of soccer are nearly unchanged from what they were 115 years ago when they were first formulated in London by the English Football Association. Known officially throughout the 142 member countries of FIFA (Federation Internationale de Football Association) as the Laws of the Game, in the United States they are habitually called the rules.

It is interesting to note also that although the FIFA rules are observed word for word throughout the rest of the world American soccer has a long tradition of tampering with them. For over 40 years colleges and high schools have altered many of the rules, and, as we will note, the NASL has seen fit to follow their lead.

The following is a review of the 17 rules, each of which has been condensed for easier reading.

Rule 1: The field of play

Figure 5.2 shows the dimensions of a soccer field. As you

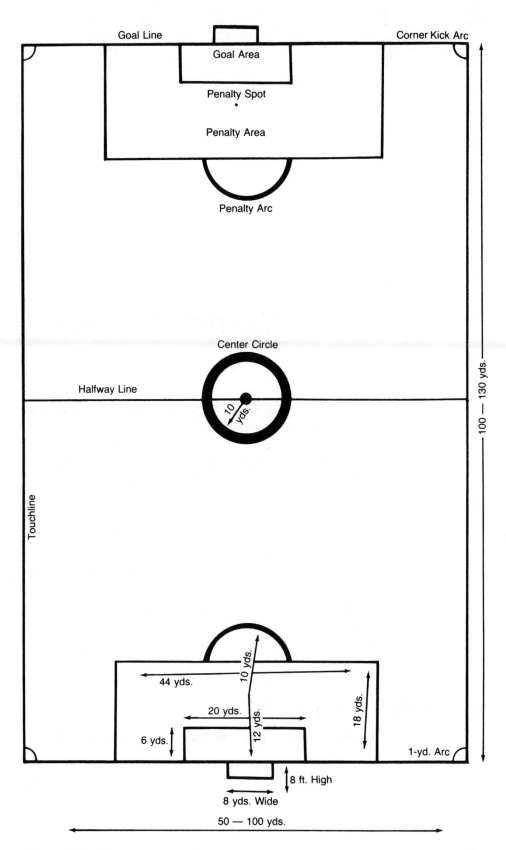

Figure 5.2:   Field of play

can see, there is great latitude as to size as long as the field is rectangular in shape, with its length greater than its breadth. FIFA does stipulate, however, that in matches between national teams of different countries the field must be 110-120 yards in length and 70-80 yards in width.

Note the large center circle and the arc adjoining the penalty area. Both are designed to keep opposing players the required ten yards from the ball at the time of kickoffs and penalty kicks.

In the NASL another line is drawn across the width of the field 35 yards from either goal line. This is the special NASL offside line marking. It is discussed under Rule 11.

In college and high school soccer in the United States the required field dimensions are as follows:

High schools—100-120 yards in length and 65-75 yards in width
Colleges—110-120 yards in length and 65-75 yards in width

Rule 2: The ball

The ball must measure between 27 and 28 inches in circumference and weigh between 14 and 16 ounces at the start of the game. At one time all balls had to be made of leather but in recent years FIFA has permitted synthetic coverings including a waterproof plastic outer coating. The NASL uses only one approved ball, made by Adidas, which is decorated with the NASL logo.

Rule 3: The number of players

This rule prescribes 11 players on a team, one of whom must be the goalkeeper. It also goes into detail about substitutions. Only two substitutes can be used in international soccer, but each national association may decide how many to allow in its own country.

One vital part of this rule that beginners should always keep in mind states that if you are ejected from a game you cannot be replaced by a substitute. However, if you are playing under United Stated college rules, a substitute could take your place provided you were not ejected for physically assaulting the referee.

The number of substitutes permitted in soccer in the United States varies from unlimited for high schools to five for colleges to only three in the NASL.

Rule 4: The player's equipment

Rule 4 deals mostly with the size of cleats (also called studs), which cannot protrude more than a quarter inch from the sole of the shoe or be smaller than half an inch in diameter.

This rule also gives the referee the right to order a player to take off anything he considers will be dangerous to another player, for example, a large ring.

Rule 4 also states that a goalkeeper must wear colors that distinguish him not only from his opponents but also from his own teammates. This means the goalie wears a different jersey or shirt from the rest of the players on the field.

Rule 5: Referees

In this rule the various duties and powers of the referee are outlined. It is made abundantly clear that he is both judge and jury. Beginners should soon learn not to argue or debate with him, since he can eject a player not only for repeated infringements of the rules but also for disrespectful or un-sportsmanlike behavior.

Another thing to bear in mind is that the referee must approve your coming onto or leaving the field on play. Don't run onto the field when you are substituted or when you have arrived at a game late without getting his attention, or else you might receive a caution.

The referee is also given the authority not to stop the game for an infringement when he believes that in stopping it he would give an advantage to the offending team. This is known throughout the soccer world as the advantage rule. The following situations are examples of when the rule would be applied: (1) when you are tackled unfairly but still manage to keep running with the ball, and (2) when you score a goal but a defender touches the ball intentionally with his hands prior to its going into the back of the net. As you can see, in either case if the referee blew his whistle and stopped play it would be unfair to your team and certainly advantageous to the offending team.

As the official timekeeper, the referee may add time lost through injury or other stoppages to the end of the game. In United States colleges and high schools, however, the referee is not the timekeeper; an appointed official performs this duty instead.

Rule 6: Linesmen

Two linesmen are required by the rules but many times in both juvenile and adult amateur soccer this requirement is waived. In colleges and high schools in the United States, instead of one referee and two linesmen there are two referees.

The duties of the linesmen require them to raise their flags to indicate to the referee when the ball has gone out of play and which team is to be awarded the restart—a throw-in, a goal kick, or a corner kick. They are also supposed to assist the referee in spotting any infringements, but the referee can, and quite often does, ignore their signaling if he so chooses.

Rule 7: Duration of the game

Although two 45-minute halves make up the official duration of the game, shorter periods are permitted for youth soccer—usually two 30-minute halves. High schools in the

United States play four quarters of not more than 18 minutes each.

Rule 7 stipulates that there must be an interval between the two halves of no more than 5 minutes unless the referee agrees to a longer rest. Generally, however, most halftimes are at least 10 minutes long.

Rule 7 also empowers the referee to extend the time of a game to permit a penalty kick to be taken.

Rule 8: The start of play

As we noted earlier, choice of ends of the field is decided by the toss of a coin, with the winning team having the alternative of either kicking off or choosing ends. If the winning team opts for the kickoff, then the other team gets the privilege of choosing ends. The team not kicking off does so at the beginning of the second half.

The rule also states that the ball is not in play at the kickoff until it has traveled the distance of its own circumference (27-28 inches), and that the kicker cannot play the ball again after the kick until some other player has touched it.

The ball must go forward from the kickoff; it cannot be passed back into your own half until the second kick or touch of the ball.

Rule 9: Ball in and out of play

There are three ways a ball can go out of play: (1) when *all of the ball* goes over the goal line; (2) when *all of the ball* goes over the touchline; and (3) when the referee stops play.

The ball remains in play if it hits the goal post, crossbar, corner flag, the referee, or a linesman as long as the ball has not gone over the goal line or touchline.

A significant point to be noted about Rule 9 is that it is not where the players are standing in relation to the touch-

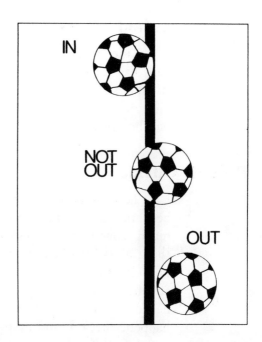

Figure 5.3: Ball in and out of play

line or goal line, but rather where the ball is, that decides if the ball is out of play or not. For example, you could dribble down the right wing and at the approach of a defender push the ball to his left while at the same time running to his right, and in doing so step over the touchline before running back to the ball. As long as the ball stayed on or inside the touchline, it would still be in play.

Another point to remember about Rule 9 is that the ball is always in play (except when it passes over one of the boundary lines) unless the referee blows his whistle. "Never stop playing until you hear the referee's whistle" has been a favorite maxim of coaches for over 100 years and still is a valid one. Even if you see what you consider to be a serious infringement committed, keep going until you hear the blast of the whistle. It may be a hand ball or a vicious kick in someone's groin; but, whatever it is, don't stop if you have the ball or are running for it, since many times the referee will wave play on because of the advantage rule.

Rule 10: Method of scoring

Rule 10 simply states that a goal is scored whenever the ball has traveled completely over the goal line. It also stipulates that a goal cannot be scored from an indirect free kick or from a throw-in unless a second player touches the ball before it crosses the goal line into the goal.

Rule 11: Offside

Traditionally, the rule determining what is offside has been the most difficult for beginners to understand. It causes much controversy even among veteran soccer buffs. One thing always to keep in mind about offside is that the rule is intended to stop any attacking player from gaining an unfair advantage over his opponents by standing in his opponents' half of the field ahead of the ball. To ensure that this does not happen, the rule states that (except as specified below) an attacker must have two opponents between him and his

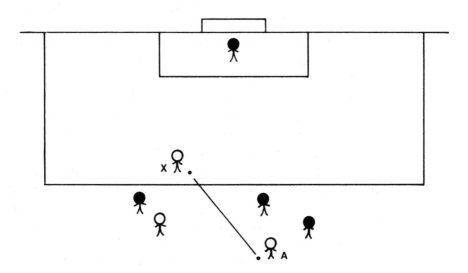

Figure 5.4: Offside when ball was passed by teammate

opponent's goal line whenever the ball is played toward him. The exceptions to this are:

1. If the player is in his own half of the field at the time the ball is played toward him
2. If the ball was last touched by an opponent
3. If the player receives the ball directly from a goal kick, corner kick, throw-in, or drop ball

Figure 5.4 shows a clear case of offside since X had only

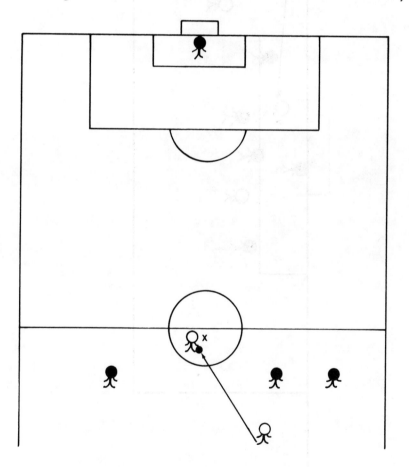

Figure 5.5: Not offside in player's half of field

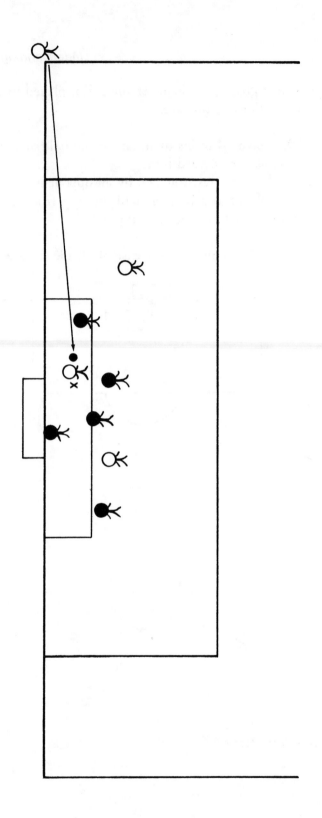

Figure 5.6: Not offside when ball came from corner kick

the goalie between him and the opponent's goal line when A passed the ball toward him.

In Figure 5.5, X is not offside since he was in his own half when the ball was passed to him. X is not offside in Figure 5.6 either, since the ball came directly from a corner kick.

In Figure 5.7, X is not offside even though he was in an offside position when the ball was played toward him because his opponent, O, in attempting to pass the ball back to his goalkeeper, was the last player to touch the ball.

One other aspect of the offside law that tends to confuse everyone is the clause that permits the referee to refrain from punishing an attacking player in an offside position if in his opinion he believes the player is not seeking to gain an advantage or is not interfering with the play. This means that

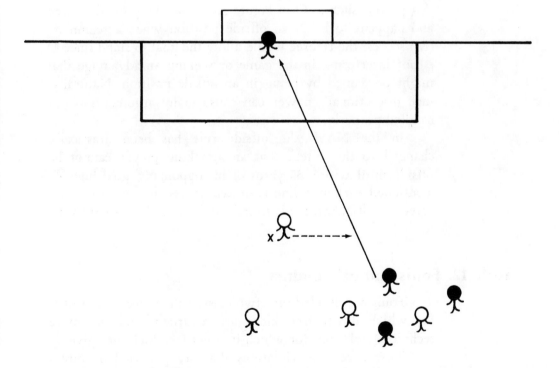

Figure 5.7: Not offside when opponent touched ball last

Figure 5.8:   Not offside when not interfering or seeking advantage

if a player, such as O in Figure 5.8, is on the ground injured and happens to be in an offside position when a teammate (M) scores, the referee would allow the goal to stand since O is not interfering in the game or seeking an advantage that might be gained by being in an offside position. Naturally, such discretionary power can cause many arguments if not handled properly.

In the NASL the offside rule has been drastically changed to the extent that an attacking player cannot be offside until within 35 yards of his opponents' goal line. As mentioned earlier, a line is drawn across the width of both halves of all NASL fields to indicate where this 35-yard zone is.

Rule 12: Fouls and misconduct

Fouls are divided into two classes: the more serious ones for which direct free kicks are awarded, and the more technical violations for which indirect free kicks are given.

There are nine violations that are punished by direct free kicks. All of them have to be committed intentionally:

1. Kicking or attempting to kick an opponent
2. Tripping an opponent
3. Jumping at an opponent
4. Charging violently at an opponent
5. Charging an opponent from behind
6. Striking or attempting to strike an opponent
7. Holding an opponent
8. Pushing an opponent
9. Handling the ball (other than the goalkeeper in his own penalty area)

Figure 5.9:   Tripping an opponent   Figure 5.10:   Holding an opponent

Indirect free kicks are awarded for the following offenses:

1. Playing in a manner considered by the referee to be dangerous (also called dangerous play) such as kicking at a shoulder-high ball when an opponent is trying to head it
2. Charging fairly but when the ball is not within playing distance (approximately within three or four feet of the players)

Figure 5.11:   Dangerous play

3. When not playing the ball, obstructing an opponent
4. Charging the goalkeeper, except when he:
   a. is holding the ball
   b. is obstructing an opponent
   c. has passed outside his goal area
5. When playing as a goalkeeper, taking more than four steps without releasing the ball, or deliberately wasting time while holding the ball

   In addition, indirect free kicks are given when the referee cautions players for the following:

1. Entering or reentering the field without permission

Figure 5.12: Obstructing an
opponent

2. Continuing to violate the rules after being cautioned
3. Arguing with the referee
4. Behaving in an ungentlemanly manner

The referee can eject players from the game for engaging in violent conduct, committing a serious foul, using obscene or abusive language, and persisting in misconduct after being cautioned.

Although not covered under Rule 12, offsides are also punished by an indirect free kick.

An important point to remember about Rule 12 is that the referee has complete discretion in deciding whether a foul is intentional or not. If, for example, a ball is kicked hard against a player's hand or arms and the referee believes the player had no intention of handling the ball, there will be no whistle on the play. Even a strong tackle that knocks an opponent down might be considered unintentional. Such discretionary power is often difficult for beginners to grasp. That is probably the reason so many of them are convinced all referees are half blind.

Some changes have been made by colleges and high schools in the above-listed FIFA rules, including a prohibition against charging goalkeepers at any time. Moreover, anyone in college or high school soccer who does charge a goalkeeper is immediately ejected from the game.

Another interesting college and high school rule bars "hitching" or "double kicking." Translated into soccer lingo, this means no overhead volleying or scissors kicking—which does seem a pity, for both are such exciting parts of soccer.

Rule 13: The free kick

Direct and indirect free kicks are explained thoroughly in this section of the rules. The more important points covered are:

1. All opponents must be ten yards away from the ball when a free kick is taken.
2. The player taking the free kick cannot play the ball again until someone else has touched it or played it.
3. When a free kick is awarded to the defending team within its own penalty area, all opponents must stay out of the penalty area until the kick is taken; and the ball must travel out of the penalty area before it is in play.

All free kicks are taken from where the infringements took place except for the direct free kick awarded against the defenders in their own penalty area, which as we noted before becomes a penalty kick.

One other important point covered in Rule 13 concerns the situation occurring when an indirect free kick is awarded to the attacking team less than ten yards from the defenders' goal line. When this happens the ten-yard rule is relaxed, and defenders may stand on their own goal line even if the indirect free kick is to be taken only four or five feet away.

Rule 14: The penalty kick

This rule prescribes that, when a penalty kick is being

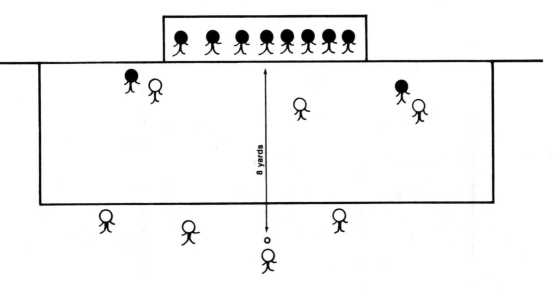

Figure 5.13:   Indirect free kick less than ten yards from goal

taken, all players other than the goalkeeper and the kicker must remain outside the penalty area. In addition, the goal-keeper must stay on his line and not move until the ball is kicked. If the goalkeeper does move before the kick is taken, it must then be retaken—unless, of course, the ball has entered the net; then the advantage rule comes into play and a goal is awarded. Similarly, if the attacking team commits an infringement, such as when one or more players come into the penalty area, then the kick has to be retaken. If a goal has been scored, it is disallowed.

Once the kick is taken any player can move into the penalty area. Players are urged to do so, since quite often the ball rebounds off the goalposts or the goalie and runs loose. One other thing to keep in mind is that as in all other free kicks the kicker cannot play the ball again until someone else, has touched it. This means that, even if the kicker's shot hits the goalpost and rebounds to him, he cannot take another shot.

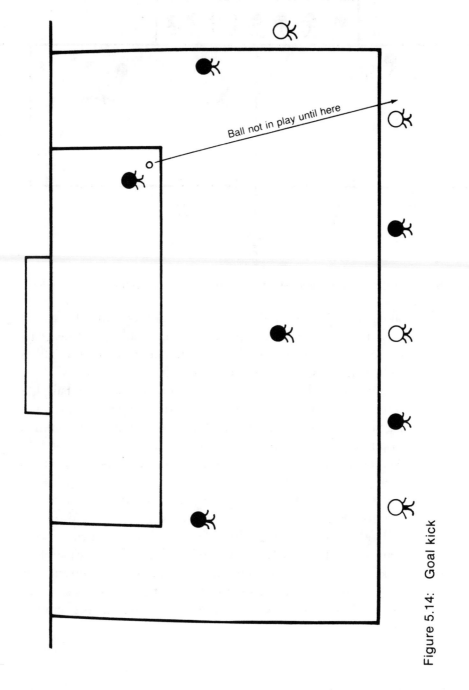

Ball not in play until here

Figure 5.14: Goal kick

Rule 15: The throw-in

This rule stipulates that for the throw-in the thrower must face the field at the moment of delivery; his feet must not step over the touchline; and the ball must be delivered from over his head.

If the throw is performed incorrectly—a foul throw—a member of the opposing team gets to take the throw.

A goal cannot be scored directly from a throw-in, and the player throwing the ball cannot play it again until someone else has touched it.

Rule 16: The goal kick

The goal kick must be taken from within the goal area, and all opponents must be out of the penalty area at the time it is taken. The ball is not in play until it passes out of the penalty area. If it is played inside the penalty area the goal kick must be retaken.

A goal cannot be scored directly from a goal kick.

Rule 17: The corner kick

Unlike in the goal kick, a goal can be scored directly from a corner kick. All opponents must stay ten yards away from the ball before it is kicked, and the kicker cannot play it again until someone else has touched it.

Photo 7:   The inimitable Pele makes one of his solo runs.

Glossary

Advantage rule—the clause found in Rule 5 giving the referee the discretionary power of disregarding a violation if he feels stopping the game would be to the advantage of the offending team.

Backs (fullbacks)—the defenders: right, center, or left backs.

Breakaway—sudden offensive movement that usually catches the defenders unprepared.

Caution—an admonishment by the referee to any player who persistently fouls or is guilty of unsportsmanlike behavior.

Center (cross)—a kick from the wing into the center of the field, usually into the opponent's penalty area, when attacking.

Center circle—the circle measuring ten yards in diameter located in the center of the field.

Charge—the shoulder charge, in which shoulder meets shoulder upon first contact between the players—the only legal charge in soccer.

Chip—a kick that enables the ball to rise rapidly.

Clearance—a kick or header by a defender that sends the ball away from the penalty area.

Corner kick—the kick awarded to the attacking team whenever a defender touches the ball last before it goes over the goal line. The kick must be taken within the corner arc, and a goal can be scored directly from it.

Cover—in soccer, cover has two meanings: (1) to guard an opponent and (2) to help a teammate by being ready to take over his defensive duties.

Dangerous play—any action by a player that the referee believes is violent or could result in an injury.

Dead ball—a ball which is not in play as a result of the referee's blowing his whistle or the ball's crossing either the touchline or the goal line.

Direct free kick—the kick awarded for the most serious infringements of the rules. A goal can be scored directly from the kick.

Distribution—another way of saying passing.

Dribbling—using the feet to advance with the ball past opponents.

Drop ball—a device used to restart the game after the referee has halted play for any reason other than an infringement of the rules. The referee drops the ball between two opponents, and the ball is not in play until it touches the ground.

European cup (the European Champion Club's Cup)—the most prestigious club tournament in the world, open to all national champions in Europe. The complete list of winners is:

1956 Real Madrid (Spain)	1968 Manchester United (England)
1957 Real Madrid	
1958 Real Madrid	1969 A.C. Milan
1959 Real Madrid	1970 Feyenoord (Netherlands)
1960 Real Madrid	
1961 Benfica (Portugal)	1971 Ajax (Netherlands)
1962 Benfica	1972 Ajax
1963 A.C. Milan (Italy)	1973 Ajax
1964 Inter Milan (Italy)	1974 Bayern Munich (West Germany)
1965 Inter Milan	
1966 Real Madrid	1975 Bayern Munich
1967 Glasgow Celtic (Scotland)	1976 Bayern Munich
	1977 Liverpool (England)

Far post—the goalpost which is the farthest from the player who has the ball.

Feint—any movement of the body with the object of confusing or misleading an opponent.

FIFA—the international body that controls world soccer. It is located in Zurich, Switzerland, and its full name is Federation Internationale de Football Association. FIFA was founded in 1904.

Forward—an offensive player; usually a winger or striker (center forward).

Foul—an infringement of the rules.

Free kick—whenever an infraction of the rules occurs a free kick is awarded against the offending team. A direct free kick is awarded for the more serious violations and an indirect for lesser ones. All free kicks are taken from the spot the infraction took place, and all opponents must be ten yards away when the kick is taken.

Goal area—the 20 by 6-yard box surrounding the goal.

Goal kick—the kick awarded to the defending team whenever the ball crosses the goal line and is last touched by an offensive player.

Goal line—the outside boundary line running along the width of the field.

Goal net—the net attached to and covering the back of the goal.

Half volley—a kick of the ball when it is rising from the ground.

Halfback—*see* Midfieldman

Halfway line—the dividing line running from one touchline to the other touchline that is an equal distance from the two goals.

Hands—a term used to describe any intentional use of the hands or arms to play the ball by any player other than the goalkeeper.

Heading—using the head to manipulate the ball.

Holding—using the hands to obstruct an opponent's movement.

Indirect free kick—a dead ball kick awarded for minor infringements of the rules. Unlike in the direct free kick, a goal cannot be scored directly from this kick.

Inswinger—a corner kick that curves toward the goal.

Interception—the cutting off of a ball intended for an opponent.

Kickoff—a kick of the dead ball from the center spot, used to start the game at the beginning of each half and to restart the game after a goal has been scored. The ball is not in play until it has traveled the distance of its own circumference (about 27–28 inches).

Lead pass—to kick or head the ball ahead of a teammate.

Linesmen—two appointed officials who assist the referee, one on each of the two touchlines. Their main task is to indicate which team should get the throw-ins, goal kicks, and corner kicks, as well as to watch for offside infractions. In addition, they alert the referee to any other infringement of the rules.

Man-to-man defense—a defensive system in which each opponent is closely marked (guarded).

Marking—guarding or shadowing an opponent.

Midfieldman—a player who acts as a link between the defensive and offensive players. Often called a halfback.

NAIA (National Association for Intercollegiate Athletics)—the athletic organization serving small colleges which has conducted a national soccer championship for its members since 1959. The winners include:

1959	Pratt Institute	1966	Quincy
1960	Elizabethtown	1967	Quincy
1961	Newark College of Engineering and Howard (co-champions)	1968	Davis and Elkins
		1969	Eastern Illinois
		1970	Davis and Elkins
1962	East Stroudsburg State	1971	Quincy
1963	Earlham College and Castleton State (co-champions)	1972	Westmont
		1973	Quincy
		1974	Quincy
1964	Trenton State	1975	Quincy
1965	Trenton State	1976	Simon Fraser

NCAA (National Collegiate Athletic Association)—the athletic association comprising the major universities and colleges in the country which runs national championships divided into three divisions:

Division one

 1959 St. Louis
 1960 St. Louis
 1961 West Chester
  State
 1962 St. Louis
 1963 St. Louis
 1964 Navy
 1965 St. Louis
 1966 San Francisco
 1967 Michigan State
  and St. Louis (co-
  champions)
 1968 Maryland and
  Michigan State (co-
  champions)
 1969 St. Louis
 1970 St. Louis
 1971 St. Louis
  (Howard won title
  but played with
  ineligible players)
 1972 St. Louis
 1973 St. Louis
 1974 Howard
 1975 San Francisco
 1976 San Francisco
 1977 Hartwick

Division two

 1971 Southern
  Illinois—
  Edwardsville
 1973 Missouri—St.
  Louis
 1974 Adelphi
 1975 Baltimore
 1976 Loyola
  (Baltimore)
 1977 Lock Haven

Division three

 1974 Brockport State
 1975 Babson College
 1976 Brandeis
 1977 Alabama A & M

NASL (North American Soccer League)—America's professional soccer circuit, formed in 1968 when the two rival pro leagues—the National Professional Soccer League and the United Soccer Association—merged following a year of disastrous financial losses. League champions have been:

1968	Atlanta Chiefs	1974	Los Angeles Aztecs
1969	Kansas City Spurs	1975	Tampa Bay Rowdies
1970	Rochester Lancers	1976	Toronto Metros-
1971	Dallas Tornado		Croatia
1972	New York Cosmos	1977	Cosmos
1973	Philadelphia Atoms		

Near post—the goalpost closest to the player with the ball.

Obstruction—a blocking of an opponent's progress with the body in order to prevent his moving with or without the ball.

Offside—the term used to describe the situation—punishable by an indirect free kick awarded to the defending team—when an offensive player is between his opponents' goal line and the ball when it is played toward him, *except when*:

1. There are two or more opponents nearer to the goal line than he is.
2. He is in his own half of the field.
3. The ball last touched an opponent.
4. He receives the ball directly from a corner kick, goal kick, throw-in, or drop ball.

Outside left—another name for left winger or left striker.

Outside right—a right winger or right striker.

Outswinger—a corner kick that curves away from the goal.

Overlapping—an offensive tactic in which defenders move up along the wings past their own forwards.

Own goal—the term used to describe the situation when a player inadvertently hits the ball past his own goalkeeper over his own goal line into the net.

Pass—to kick or head the ball from one player to another.

Penalty area—the 44 by 18-yard box directly in front of the goal.

Penalty kick—a direct free kick awarded to the offensive team in the defenders' penalty area.

Penalty spot—the mark 12 yards from the goal from which the penalty kicks are taken.

Pitch—another name for the field, originating in Britain.

Punt—a goalkeeper's kick used for long clearances. The ball is dropped from the hands and kicked with the instep.

Running off the ball—running without the ball in order to support a teammate with the ball or to seek an unguarded area where a pass can be received.

Save—any catch, punch, or deflection made by the goalkeeper.

Screening—legally using the body to prevent an opponent from reaching the ball.

Shot—any kick or heading of the ball at your opponents' goal.

Shoulder charge—*see* Charge.

Striker—the modern name for center forward; also refers to any forward.

Sweeper—a defender who plays behind the rest of the defense.

Tackling—using the feet to take the ball away from an opponent.

Ten-yard rule—a rule that states all players must be at least ten yards from the ball when a free kick or a corner kick is awarded against their team. The only exception to this rule is when an indirect free kick is awarded less than ten yards from the defending team's goal line.

Throw-in—the method of restarting the game whenever the ball has crossed a touchline. A player throws the ball into the field from outside the touchline where the ball went out of play.

Touchlines—the outside boundary lines running along the length of the field. Often called the sidelines.

Trapping—using the feet, thighs, chest, or head to stop a moving ball.

USSF (the United States Soccer Federation)—the governing body of United States soccer. The USSF was founded in 1913 and is a member of FIFA. The organization's original name was USFA (United States Football Association). In 1945 it was changed to USSFA (United States Soccer Football Association), and in 1974 its present name was adopted.

Volley—a kick of a moving ball that is up off the ground.

Wall pass—a pass to a teammate who returns it to you so that you can run past an intervening opponent and collect the ball in an unguarded space. Your teammate actually follows a path like the straight line of a wall. The wall pass is also called the give-and-go.

Wing—the area along the touchline (approximately 15-20 yards wide).

Wingers—the outside strikers. Also called outside right and outside left.

World cup—the official world championship for the 142 nations that belong to FIFA. The World Cup competition has been held once every four years, except when World War II intervened. Past champions are:

1930	Uruguay	1958	Brazil
1934	Italy	1962	Brazil
1938	Italy	1966	England
1950	Uruguay	1970	Brazil
1954	West Germany	1974	West Germany

Zone defense—a defensive system in which .each member patrols an assigned area.

Index